**Tanouki**

I0560626

# God
# ex nihilo

## The paradox of creation

### Beliefs, atheism
### and representations

**Relectures**

# Summary

# Foreword

God: to believe or not to believe?

Is this really the dilemma?

Isn't the real question rather "Does God exist?", or more precisely "Does an entity called God exist?"

The issue is therefore existential.

However, existence is either factual or hypothetical. But all hypotheses inevitably refer to facts.

This is why the philosophers of monotheistic religions, who were often more theologians than philosophers, have always sought arguments in reason in favor of a single god, if not proof of his existence.

The method was nevertheless always philosophical, or more precisely theological. Theology starts from the existence of God as a prerequisite for any intellectual endeavor, whether philosophical or scientific.

Science, the domain of facts, remained subject to theology, the guardian of knowledge, for a long time. Over the centuries, it finally broke free, to the point of gaining a virtual monopoly on knowledge and therefore on facts.

It was then that certain contemporary authors, convinced of the existence of God, began to question science in the hope of finding confirmation, or even proof.

However, this approach misses the fundamental and therefore primary question: What is God?

Is there a coherent answer to this question?

This is what we need to determine by examining the conceptions of God given by monotheistic religions, but also by reading the efforts of certain theologians to resolve the inconsistencies that inevitably arise upon initial analysis. Can they convince us?

In the last century, Daniel Massé said that theology was « *l'art de prendre et de faire prendre des vessies pour des lanternes* » (the art of taking a pig in a poke.) Was he entirely wrong?

It's up to everyone to judge.

Opposite belief in God are a number of philosophical positions, or considered as such, the most categorical of which is atheism.

What is atheism? And what is it not?

By seeing atheism as merely a philosophical trend or a social project, as some authors suggest, are we not overlooking a new form of atheism that is more common, more widespread, and perhaps unshakable, and which continues to grow?

Should we oppose it with Paule Levers' assertion that God is "the fundamental desire of all consciousness"?

This short book attempts to answer all these questions in a simple way, appealing to the common sense that everyone possesses. There is no need to get lost in a display of knowledge, as in those endless books. A few quotes from the most influential authors will suffice. They will give an idea of what has been said and what is being said.

Anyway, what matters here is to get to the heart of the matter.

# Does God exist?

Does God exist?

Is this really a question we ask ourselves?

In general, it is more like, "Do you believe in God?" or "Do I believe in God?"

One might legitimately think that the answers to these two questions also answer the first. However, they only answer the question "Do you believe that God exists?" or "Do I believe that God exists?" We are therefore still in the realm of belief, i.e., in a priori acceptance or rejection. However, here, it is not so much a question of belief as of existence.

And why God with a capital letter? Shouldn't we ask a more neutral question: "Is there a god?" or "Do you believe in a god?"

This is because, in general, the question asked concerns the God of monotheism, who is well defined and whom everyone has heard of to some extent or another or has been raised within one of the three monotheistic religions.

The question "Does God exist?" therefore seems legitimate and should it not be the only possible question? Similarly, it is not a question of whether or not we believe in extraterrestrials, but whether extraterrestrials exist, or, more precisely, whether it is possible that extraterrestrial beings exist.

Most of the time, to answer this question, we look for answers or arguments in philosophy or science.

But what person, believer or non-believer, even slightly educated, even in possession of all the qualifications necessary to form a clear judgment, is capable of ingesting and digesting the imposing body of often indigestible texts that few have read, apart from doctoral students and professional philosophers? Plato, Aristotle, Augustine of Hippo, Thomas Aquinas, Descartes, Spinoza, Kant, Hegel, Schopenhauer, Nietzsche ; to name but a few of the authors, the least recent ones, who populate the pantheon of philosophers, who are called upon to answer questions about the existence of God.. Not to mention references to the most recent scientific discoveries and hypotheses, which are more or less well understood and sometimes completely outdated by the time they are referred to.

Most contemporary authors who address the problem of God's existence get lost in quotations and analyses that overwhelm the average reader, who, often unable to judge the validity of these analyses, either gives up reading halfway through, skims through and accepts the conclusions that confirm their beliefs, or, unconvinced, rejects them outright.

Nevertheless, once the question has been asked, we cannot avoid examining the concept, the very idea, of this God of monotheism. Is not the first question we must ask, if not answer, at least attempt to answer, "What exactly is God?"

According to the philosopher Michel Meyer, "*What could be more natural, at the outset, than to question the starting point? Isn't this question, by definition, the first of all? But who begins anything by asking it? Isn't the answer considered obvious? [...] The case of the axiom seems exemplary: what could be more indisputably first than it? That would be to forget that it is only there to justify. It only becomes apparent in retrospect. If it is first, it is only in relation to what follows, but it is what follows that allows us to discover it. This amounts to concluding that, in order to know a starting point, even one as certain as an axiom, we must first discover what it is, which is paradoxical if it is supposed to be the thing that, in good logic, gives access to everything else and precedes it.*[1]

Replace the word "axiom" with "God" and we are faced with a problem that bears great similarities.

Is not God, for all theistic religions, whether polytheistic or monotheistic, the first axiom?

However, God, to consider only the monotheistic God[2] , is, at first glance, only conceivable through the attributes we give him and the actions we attribute to him.

Consequently, while there are different ways of approaching the problem of God's existence, one approach seems particularly legitimate, and that is to question the very concept of God.

But how can we question such a being about which we have no direct knowledge and which is the subject of a belief in which reason often has little place and which is not, strictly speaking, a hypothesis? Black holes are a hypothesis, or at least they were until

---

[1] Michel Meyer, *Questionnement et historicité* (Questioning and historicity), Quadrige collection, PUF, chapter 1, *La question du questionnement* (The question of questioning), p. 7

[2] Throughout this text, the word "god," when not preceded by a determiner and thus referring to the god of monotheism, will begin with a capital letter, because, being unique and personal, the term becomes a kind of proper name designating a unique being.

recently, in the field of astrophysics, which requires special knowledge and skills. Nothing of the sort applies to God, who only becomes a hypothesis when the concept, and therefore the attributes that define it, are put to the test of logic. This is a very simple logic that does not require scientific theories or abstruse philosophical or theological reflections. It is a logic that is accessible to everyone and, it should be emphasized, was not foreign to the meditations of medieval thinkers.

The most direct way to question the existence of this God, this being whom we worship, whom we cannot explain, but who is at the center and origin of monotheistic religions, is therefore to question his attributes.

But, posing the problem of his existence is also, through the examination of his attributes, questioning his credibility: is he plausible? And beyond that, it is the degree of acceptability of this concept of a single god that is called into question.

First of all, what kind of being are we talking about? What are its attributes? In short, when we say "God," what are we talking about?

# The god of monotheism: what is it all about?

This god, who is said to be indefinable and neither provable nor disprovable, is nevertheless traditionally thought of as a personal, immaterial, unique, eternal, all-powerful being and creator of all things.

What is the precise meaning of each of these attributes, and what do they imply?

The uniqueness of God means that he is alone in his state, the only one to possess his attributes.

To say that God is a personal being is to affirm that he is not a celestial body, like the sun, that he cannot be equated with nature, that he is a being endowed with consciousness and will. The notion of being personal, associated with that of immateriality, refers to the notion of pure spirit and therefore to that of a purely "mental" entity[3] . One could also say that he is pure thought, even if this expression is a little awkward.

Eternity means the absence of beginning and end, and therefore the absence of temporality.

The term creator implies that it pre-exists its creation, omnipotence indicates that it is the cause of all things, and, when combined with its uniqueness, this means that it is the All, that nothing exists outside of it "before" creation.

Let us also specify that by "everything" we mean not only everything that constitutes the universe we know

---

[3] Although the term "mental" is undoubtedly ambiguous here insofar as it applies in principle to a human being, and therefore to a material being, it nevertheless facilitates the representation of what a pure spirit might be in the sense given by religions.

with its space-time, but also what makes this universe exist and, by extrapolation, the fact that there is being, independently of our universe (if there can be anything else) and independently of the divine being itself.

Isn't creation the first act that defines the god of monotheism? Isn't the attribute of creator at the root of our idea of god, giving him or her omnipotence?

The text of Genesis, which opens the Bible, the sacred book from which monotheistic religions developed and which is still considered by many to be a fundamental text, clearly shows that the concept of creation is essential to the idea of God and that, without this concept, God would have no substance or even any reason to exist.

The first sentence of the Christian creed affirms this:

"*I believe in God, the Father almighty, creator of heaven and earth.*"

Emil Brunner, Swiss pastor and theologian (1889-1966), confirms this: "*To say that God brought the world out of nothing is to assert first of all that God is God. [...] It is only because and to the extent that he creates out of nothing that the creator God is sovereign.*"[4]

Has this concept become outdated? For some contemporary Christian thinkers and theologians, this seems to be the case, because if we examine it more closely, is the idea of creation compatible with the other

---

[4] Emil Brunner, trans. Étienne Trocmé, *La Doctrine chrétienne du Dieu Créateur* (The Christian Doctrine of the Creator God), Revue d'histoire et de philosophie religieuses, 34th year no 4,1954, pp. 333 and 334

attributes of this unique, personal, eternal, timeless, immaterial, and almighty god?

To get a better idea, let's examine each of these attributes in relation to the others.

First, we are faced with the assertion of creation by a personal, immaterial being out of nothing. This is what the expression "ex nihilo" emphasizes: out of nothing. Nothing is also what we call nothingness.

But what is nothingness?

Far from being an empty space, as a simplistic imagination would have it, because space is still something, nothingness implies a total absence of being. This is difficult to imagine since, by definition, we cannot have a representation of non-being.

Playing with words, we could say that before creation, God is present in absence. Or, to put it another way, we would have to accept the idea that outside of creation, this one God is a conscious entity present in non-being, or that non-being contains consciousness. Both statements are equally absurd, since the ideas of content or presence only apply to being. Saying that God is "a purely mental entity in nothing" does not solve the problem either. And it is pointless to add "nowhere," since "nothing" implies the absence of space-time, and therefore of place.

One might respond that the question of God's existence should not be posed in this way, since God is being itself, indeed the supreme being. We will then conclude that the concept of nothingness has no legitimacy, that it is pure intellectual speculation, that there has always been being since in the beginning there was God, who is eternal and who therefore represented all being, meaning that there was nothing outside of him. It is then the notion of creation ex nihilo that also loses all meaning.

At this stage of reflection, we still do not understand anything.

To sum up, it is difficult to imagine a consciousness in the absence of anything else, especially material substance. We are, a priori, faced with an incomprehensible being.

At this stage of reflection, it is not forbidden to consider such an entity as either absurd or purely abstract, because it is difficult, if not impossible, to conceive of it.

Nevertheless, it must be acknowledged that for most believers, if not the majority, the existence of God as a prerequisite for all material existence presents no difficulty. Whether they have a naive and anthropomorphic conception of God, or whether they consider that God is beyond comprehension, in other words that God does not need to be understood or explained, but that God's existence must be accepted without further consideration, sometimes with a so-called spiritual approach.

The problem raised here is that of representation.
What is representation?

# Belief and representations

Representation is a mental image that allows us to conceive or visualize something or someone that is absent, or something abstract or non-existent, but which can be linked to concrete people or things. A carpenter has a mental representation of the table he wants to make. An artist conceives his drawing before he creates it; he visualizes it mentally (In other words: he has a mental representation of his drawing). We can imagine a unicorn, a horse with a horn in the middle of its forehead, because we know what a horse and a horn are. We can also have a representation of wickedness or kindness by remembering or imagining a person who has behaved in a way that we would describe as wicked or kind.

But to conceive of a being that is purely spirit, eternal, unique, and the totality of all that exists, and what is more, capable of producing energy and matter from nothing, is simply impossible. Either we accept this as a pure and indisputable truth, or the mind stumbles and cannot integrate this idea. One can, of course, extrapolate from a human being who has attained perfection in all areas and who has no body. This is how the imagination creates angels, jinn, and other spirits such as demons. But these are anthropomorphic representations. We imagine the devil as an evil and malicious person and God as a father, a being endowed with human feelings. But this is a naive conception.

The question that arises here is whether we can

speak of belief, or faith, in the total absence of representations of the object of that belief.

Is it possible to think God without mental representations?

Even if we must assume his existence as something a priori beyond human understanding, he is determined by his attributes, which revolve around his status as creator, at the very heart of his definition. For although there is no true definition (in the precise sense of the term) of God, he is nevertheless defined by his attributes. It cannot be otherwise. Can we believe in something that is not, to some extent, determined? Thus, we are entitled to consider that the attributes we give him define him.

However, if we need to examine God's attributes in order to understand Him, these attributes cannot be understood without their representations. To understand this, let us examine some of these attributes in relation to the concept of creation.

## An eternal being who created the world
### the contradictions the paradox

Let us examine the ideas of an eternal being, that is, the idea of eternity in relation to that of creation.

The idea of "world," which in ancient times corresponded to our earth and the universe of which it was supposed to be the center, must be expanded (as we said earlier) not only to the entire universe, but to all substance, including energy, at the origin of the universe, in particular that which could exist beyond this universe of ours and which causes it to exist (the creation of the world meaning the creation of everything that is not God himself).

Thus, this one God is, by his eternal nature, without past or future, in an absolute present. Eternity, in the total absence of beings other than God himself, implies the absence of temporality.

He is alone, eternal, and all-powerful: to say that he is content with simply being is an understatement; he exhausts himself in his very being. And to say this is to say that he has no need to create space-time or other beings, since by definition he is self-sufficient. He is the All.

Thus, it is not forbidden to assert that the concept of creation is a negation of eternity and therefore of God as eternal.

To understand this, we must adopt a more naive view of what the idea of creation represents in relation to that of eternity. Thus, if we were to reason like a child who has received no religious education, who is ignorant even of the idea of God, and to whom a reckless adult undertakes to teach the rudiments of belief, we might ask the following question:

"But when did this god decide to create the world, and why at that precise moment, why not before or later?"

*"God gave birth to time. Before Creation, time did not exist. That is why the question, 'What was God doing before Creation?' is a stupid question. It is Creation that brings about the existence of a before and an after."*[5] Replied Swiss pastor and theologian Emil Brunner in the last century, simply repeating what Augustine of Hippo (Saint Augustine) had said fifteen centuries earlier[6].

"Good answer!" one might say, given that eternity implies the absence of time, and therefore there is no "before" or "after."

However, this is only apparent stupidity.

To understand this, we need to think carefully about what the concept of eternity means. Either we see it as the perhaps simplistic but common representation of an

---

[5] Emil Brunner, trans. Étienne Trocmé, *La Doctrine chrétienne du Dieu Créateur,* Revue d'histoire et de philosophie religieuses, 34th year, no 4, 1954, p. 331-332

[6] *"A light-hearted mind may already be rushing into an imaginary past of centuries, and be surprised that the Almighty, creator and preserver of the world, the architect of heaven and earth, has allowed an ocean of infinite ages to flow by without undertaking this great work. Let him wake from his slumber and consider the futility of his astonishment! For whence would have come this course of countless centuries if you had not been their author, you, the author and founder of the centuries? What time could there have been without your institution? And how would it have passed, this time that could not have been?"* Augustine of Hippo, *Confessions* - Book Eleven - Chapter XIII, translated by M. Moreau (1864)

infinity of moments strung together, in which case considerations of a before and after are perfectly justified; or, considering this mental construct to be erroneous, we replace it with the undoubtedly more accurate idea of the "total present." That is to say, the absence of past and future. And then everything becomes complicated. Because with the total present, everything freezes. Action does not exist and cannot exist. Action is inseparable from temporality, especially since it presupposes will, which precedes action. And God's action par excellence, which makes him what he is, is creation.

Thus, this creator god would introduce a point of impact on this eternity that he would annihilate by creating the instant, with an "after" and therefore a "before." This zero instant, hooked onto eternity, alters it by introducing an "after," which presupposes a "before."

Here we are also faced with a problem of representation. Thus, if we consider the idea of eternity, not as an infinity of moments or as a continuous line that has no limit, but as a total present (absence of past and future), it is difficult to imagine a zero moment as the starting point of a temporality created from this total present. We remain in the realm of purely abstract notions that cannot be represented and cannot in any way be deduced from astrophysical theories such as the Big Bang, as some authors do in order to give the idea of creation a semblance of rationality.[7]

---

[7] It should be noted that the concepts of time and eternity differ profoundly depending on philosophical, theological, or scientific perspectives. In mathematics, the term infinity is used. Time and eternity are therefore delicate concepts to handle.

The God hypothesis, not to say the God axiom, posits a punctual beginning of time from an absolute present. The punctuality of the beginning of time is not the subject of any astrophysical conclusion; the big bang theory only talks about singularity. Stephen Hawking and Leonard Mlodinow confirm this:

"B*ut although one can think of the big bang picture as a valid description of early times, it is wrong to take the big bang literally, that is, to think of Einstein's theory as providing a true picture of the origin of the universe. That is because general relativity predicts there to be a point in time at which the temperature, density, and curvature of the universe are all infinite, a situation mathematicians call a singularity. To a physicist this means that Einstein's theory breaks down at that point and therefore cannot be used to predict how the universe began, only how it evolved afterward. So although we can employ the equations of general relativity and our observations of the heavens to learn about the universe at a very young age, it is not correct to carry the big bang picture all the way back to the beginning.* »[8]

Returning to the theistic hypothesis of creation, eternity is God himself and nothing else. Creation draws him into this temporality that he has unfortunately created. For if this temporality were independent of him, we would then be justified in doubting that he was its creator. Furthermore, his direct or indirect interventions within his creation, the temporality of which cannot be questioned by believers, are undeniable indications of his temporal intrusions. Is it not precisely the three great monotheistic religions that tell us this: the interventions of God recounted in the Bible are numerous; among Christians, the date of

[8] Stephen Hawking and Leonard Mlodinow, *The Grand Design*, In the chapter *"Choosing Our Universe* »

birth of Jesus Christ (the incarnation of God) and that of his death, even if approximate and uncertain, are the subject of debate; similarly, the inspirations of the prophet of Islam, whose dates should not be a problem for Muslims.

Thus, the question "What was the Son of God doing before Jesus Christ appeared on earth?" is not devoid of common sense or logic. Should we answer "nothing," as Saint Augustine did when asked "What was God doing before creation?"

From a logical point of view, God is intrinsically linked to the temporality he created. Isn't this creation of time a corruption of God's eternity?

Furthermore, the concept of creation also refers to the notion of contingency, which describes that which may or may not be, i.e., that which is not necessary. This notion is therefore incompatible with that of eternity, since that which is eternal is, by definition, necessary.

On the other hand, creation can only produce contingency since no necessity is attached to it. In other words, God, who is already the Whole and therefore has no need for creation in order to exist, ipso facto creates contingency.

At this stage of reflection, we are faced with several contradictions. First, is the notion of contingency compatible with the idea of the oneness of God? Since being the All, what he creates should inevitably be part of himself[9]. Nevertheless, being already totality, he

---

[9] As we have seen above, since the concept of nothingness has no meaning, since there has always been something (God himself), we must therefore conclude that God creates from himself.

cannot increase his divine being.. Moreover, he cannot introduce contingence within himself, which would be contradictory with regard to his divine nature.

But denying that his creation is part of himself in that he is not in what he creates, according to the principle that every creature is, a priori, independent of its creator, and that, on the other hand, he cannot introduce contingency into himself, leads to the conclusion that he is no longer the Whole, since the Whole cannot be increased by something that is not part of it.

It would then have to be considered that God deliberately divested himself, in either case, of his divine character, since he annihilates his timelessness, and therefore the eternal nature of his being, his totality, and his omnipotence, since what is contingent exists independently of him.

It should also be noted that the concept of creation suggests the idea of desire, in the sense of wanting something that one does not have or that does not exist, a priori. This concept is incompatible with that of an eternal and omnipotent god. It is generally replaced by the concept of will. Thus, creation is the result of God's will. However, since God's will is necessary (a necessity of consequence, as Thomas Aquinas points out, not a conditional necessity[10] ), creation therefore necessarily exists and cannot be considered contingent. This contradicts the above and also implies that, since God's will is eternal, creation is also eternal. We would

---

[10] Necessity of consequence characterizes what a thing is by nature, while conditional necessity means that without one thing, another thing cannot happen (eyes are necessary for vision).

then have to conclude that God has been creating for all eternity, which would mean that time has existed for all eternity (since it is an integral part of creation), which is contradictory in itself, but also with the idea of creation ex nihilo.

We would then have to conclude that the concept of creation is incompatible with the idea of a god possessing the attributes attributed to him by monotheistic religions.

However, as previously emphasized and confirmed by theologian Emil Brunner, God cannot not have created. In other words, God is only God because he created. Without creation, God is no longer a deity.

Thus, the notion of creation in relation to the notions of uniqueness, immateriality, eternity, and omnipotence is based on a whole set of contradictions that lead to a paradox: the "paradox of creation." This also means that God is an eminently paradoxical being.

These reflections echo the words of philosopher Vincent Citot: "*In the strict sense, God is nothing other than the Absolute as such. That religions need to humanize God by imagining him with a beard, sitting on a throne somewhere in the sky, watching over mankind, cursing, scolding, or rewarding, is their business. This passionate and anxious God, however, is a man! The idea of God is the idea of the Absolute, of that which is not relative, of that which does not need to be in relation to anything in order to exist and which, as a result, is in relation to nothing, is in relation only to itself, enjoying itself eternally without distance or difference. But this is unthinkable, for an obvious reason: thought itself introduces this forbidden difference. To think is to analyze, connect, objectify, cut up, and piece together: thought excludes, in its very being, that it can be thought of God. To think God is to kill God; it is to make him a contradictory object. "* [11]

In short, if there is a god, he can only be the creator of all that is, which is nevertheless incompatible with his nature. He therefore appears as a purely fictional being, whose existence is impossible.

The incompatibility of the concept of creation with that of God would thus lead to the conclusion that there was no creation, and therefore no God either. And if we were to claim to see any proof of this, we could formulate it as follows : *the very fact that there is being is the ultimate proof that God does not exist.*

To put it more simply: *the existence of the universe proves the non-existence of God.*

In reality, rather than proving the non-existence of God, this is a matter of showing that the classical representations of the attributes that define him do not hold water, to put it bluntly.

Of course, we can consider all this to be a mind game, a juggling act with concepts and logic, and remain at the level of pure intellectual speculation based on naive representations.

---

[11] Vincent Citot, *La tentation métaphysique et l'exigence philosophique* (The metaphysical temptation and the philosophical requirement), magazine, Le Philosophoire 1999/3 no 9, article, La Métaphysique (available at Cairn.info), p. 67

No doubt, but it is speculation that uses logic to question another speculation, which is itself built on a completely different logic where abstract images and feelings take precedence over reason. As for the supposedly naive representations, if they have been and still are contested by many theologians, it is because they are effective and are held by the vast majority of believers.

One could also object that the logic underlying this line of reasoning is entirely human, and that God is precisely beyond the human, beyond human logic, beyond even all logic. But if that is the case, then human concepts have no legitimacy in defining the attributes of God. This would amount to what is known as negative theology (also called apophatic theology), which consists in saying that God is neither this nor that, nor anything that can be imagined, based on the principle of *"the fundamental inadequacy of our representations and statements in relation to the mystery of God."*[12] .

This is what Yves Tesmontant set out to explain to us in the last century[13] ):

*"The representations of God suggested by the behavior of those who pronounce this name, or by so-called 'religious' teaching, certainly also play a major role, as obstacles, in the repulsion that so many of our*

---

[12] Charles Wackenheim, *Actualité de la théologie négative* (The Relevance of Negative Theology), Revue des Sciences Religieuses, vol. 59, fascicule 2, 1985, p. 147

[13] Yves Tesmontant, *Comment se pose aujourd'hui le problème de l'existence de Dieu* (How the Problem of God's Existence Arises Today), 1966, epilogue, p. 399

26

*contemporaries—often among the best—feel toward their idea of God. Yet the entire biblical tradition, both Jewish and Christian, insists on repeating that there is no representation of God. Any representation of God is inevitably an obstacle, anthropomorphism, and idolatry. Orthodox Christian theology and mysticism repeat the same thing: representations, whether visual or emotional, must be eliminated. The living God is a hidden God. [...] And that is precisely why it is so important, so urgent, to develop today a theology of creation, redemption, and sin that is free from the infantile and neurotic representations that too often envelop it in common teaching.*

The author is referring here to anthropomorphic representations, which he describes as childish. However, God possesses attributes that are also representations insofar as they are understood by analogy with concrete situations experienced in life.

Eternity, as pointed out above, can only be understood through the concepts of time and aging. The concept of pure spirit can be understood through the mental activity that everyone possesses, by imagining the continuation of this faculty despite the disappearance of the body. The concept of creation is also understandable by analogy with the activities involved in making objects, or more simply by analogy with the gestation and birth of a human being. The love we attribute to God is the ultimate affective representation:

*"Let us be aware that we are constantly developing representations of the divine based on our own desires. If we conceive of a God who is omniscient and omnipotent, even infinitely good, is this not an*

*expression of what we aspire to?"*[14]

François-Xavier PUTALLAZ, A Swiss PHILOSOPHER, nevertheless attempts to convince us of the falsity of representations of creation:

*"What is creation? It is not an emanation like the sun emanating its light; it is the emanation of everything that is, of all being and everything in being, from the universal cause that is God, and from nothing. And what is striking is that we will always be incapable of conceiving of creation. Because what we have as experience is always the transformation of the sculptor, it is always generation, and it is always emanation that we experience. So there is an inevitable illusion, to use Bergson's term, whenever we talk about creation, in that we will rely on one of these three experiences and we must constantly strive to say: creation from nothing is neither a transformation nor a generation nor an emanation.*[15]

Thus, we can say what creation is not, but it is impossible to say what it is. This amounts to saying that we cannot have any representation of it, or at least that the representations we have are all erroneous, which amounts to the same thing. To this, one might object that we always have representations; that is largely how

---

[14] François Euvé, *La science, l'épreuve de Dieu* (In French, a play on words between "l'épreuve" (the test) and "les preuves" (the evidences), a review of the book by Michel-Yves Bolloré and Olivier Bonnassies *Dieu la science les preuves* (God, the Science, the Evidence)

[15] François-Xavier Putallaz, speech on iaquinas.com and reposted on YouTube, "*Qu'est-ce qu'on appelle création ex nihilo ?*" (What is creation ex nihilo?) (I, 45-46) https://www.youtube.com/watch?v=s7HC3idJXQ0

the human brain works. This is also what François-Xavier Putallaz observes, since he takes the trouble to specify that these are false representations, precisely because they are not only widely shared, but because they are the only representations possible for ordinary people.

On the other hand, God's attributes inevitably give rise to representations, which are in fact one of the essential components of religious belief, according to Yves Lambert (a sociologist specializing in the sociology of religion):

*"A religious belief can be seen as a representation of a supra-empirical reality that is supposed to be at the origin of empirical reality, with which it is possible to communicate."*[16]

Thus, rejecting all representations would ultimately mean rejecting all attributes of God, which would imply rejecting any definition of God, which would be absurd. Need we repeat it: one cannot believe in something that is not, more or less, clearly defined.

The god of monotheism is therefore defined, relatively clearly, by the attributes we give him, first and foremost his attribute as creator. Thus, God is only understandable through his attributes, which are all representations. This also means that he can only be conceived through his representations. He is his representations. He is representation.

To see any naivety in working on concepts and definitions that have been largely superseded by many

---

[16] Yves Lambert, *La naissance des religions* (The Birth of Religions), p. 29

contemporary theologians and thinkers is to forget that, on the one hand, these representations have functioned for centuries and still function today, regardless of the beliefs of believers, and that, on the other hand, theologians, whether Jewish, Muslim, or Christian, were not unaware of these contradictions and have strived to resolve them. We will have the opportunity to return to this in the following pages.

It is worth noting here that the acceptance of the theory of evolution by most theologians is in no way an abandonment of the concept of creation, as God is still considered the master of this evolution and remains, in all cases, the origin of being and of a transcendent nature. His status as creator is therefore not called into question.

Apart from the followers of creationism or intelligent design, who are mainly found in the United States, the majority of Christians seem to adhere to the theory of evolution. The Catholic Church has almost officially accepted it through Pope John Paul II, who recognized that this theory was "more than a hypothesis."

This position is not new, according to this text published in *La Revue d'histoire et de philosophie religieuses* in 1954: "*The scientific doctrine of evolution has no bearing whatsoever on belief in Creation, whether for or against it. It is silent on the subject of Creation; it speaks only of changes that have occurred within the created world. [...] This question (*the evolution of species) *is of no interest to theology, which cannot provide any answer to it. It belongs to the realm of knowledge about the world, not to that of faith.* »[17]

---

[17] Emil Brunner, trans. Étienne Trocmé. *La Doctrine chrétienne du Dieu Créateur* (The Christian Doctrine of the Creator God), Revue d'histoire et de philosophie religieuses, 34th year, no 4, 1954, p. 336

# Theology and the paradox

Theologians of the three monotheistic religions, who have focused their reflections on the problem raised by the concepts of creation and eternity, were well aware of the incompatibility of these two notions and have strived to provide various theological explanations for the sake of intellectual consistency.

This is not the place to review exhaustively the different points of view of theologians throughout the ages. The most representative figures will suffice.

The spread of the ideas of certain Greek philosophers, especially Aristotle, led medieval theologians to examine the question of whether the world was eternal or not, which was linked to the question of creation. Some Muslim thinkers (such as Averroes and Avicenna), aware of the contradictions inherent in the concept of creation and starting from the principle that an eternal cause can only produce eternal effects, considered the world to be eternal, and therefore to have always existed. This contradicts the idea that creation presupposes the pre-existence of the creator in relation to his creation. Thus, the world, coexisting with God, who is no longer its creator, is not contingent. In doing so, believing they were resolving a paradox, they created another one, which moreover left the field open to the proponents of pantheism, who considered that God and the world are one, and to those of atheism, who were inclined to deduce from this the uselessness of God, and therefore his non-existence.

The considerations of Muslim philosophers in their

commentaries on Aristotle's writings triggered what became known as the "Controversy over the Eternity of the World" among Christians in the Middle Ages. Some were for it, others against it.

Thomas Aquinas resolved this paradox by taking an agnostic stance on the eternity of the world, considering that it was not possible to conclude either for or against its eternity, but that the idea of eternal creation (in other words, a world eternally created by God) was not contradictory.

Regarding the problem of contingency, which, as we discussed above, would seem to contradict God's will (necessary will), Thomas asserts that "*the divine will does not remove contingency from things nor impose absolute necessity on them*" because "*God wills that there be contingent beings.*" There is therefore no need to ponder the matter. There is no contradiction; it is God who willed it so!

As for the problem of creation ex nihilo, the Swiss philosopher François-Xavier Putallaz explains the Thomist point of view:

"*When we use this term, we are subject to illusion. We have the impression that first there is nothing and then there is something. But this is an illusion, since if there is nothing, this nothing cannot precede what exists. So there is no anteriority in terms of duration or temporality of nothingness, followed by something. Therefore, ex nihilo does not mean that there is nothing and then something, but rather an anteriority of nature. It means that the world is suspended by God's eternal creative act and held above nothingness.*"[18]

A Jewish theologian, Isaac Louria (1534-1572), introduced the concept of tsimtsoum (withdrawal or contraction) to resolve the incompatibility between the concept of creation and that of En sof (unlimited, infinite).

The concept of tsimtsum is explained by Marc-Alain Ouaknin, philosopher and rabbi:

*"Rabbi Isaac Luria asked himself the following questions:*
- *How can there be a world if God is everywhere?*
- *If God is 'All in all', how can there be things that are not God?*
- *How can God create the world ex nihilo, if there is no nothingness?*

*Rabbi Isaac Louria responded by formulating the theory of Tsimtsoum or "withdrawal." According to this theory, the Creator's first act was not to reveal himself to something external. Far from being a movement outward or a departure from his hidden identity, the first step was a withdrawal; God withdrew "from himself into himself" and, by this act, left a void, a place within himself, creating space for the world to come.*

*At a certain point within the light of the Infinite (En sof), the divine essence or "light" eclipsed itself; a space was left empty in the middle. In relation to the Infinite, this space was no more than an infinitesimal point, but in relation to Creation, it was the entire*

---

[18] François-Xavier Putallaz, speech on iaquinas.com and reposted on YouTube, "Q*u'est-ce qu'on appelle création ex nihilo ?*" (What is creation ex nihilo?) (I, 45-46):
https://www.youtube.com/watch?vs7hc3idjxq0

*cosmic space. God could only manifest himself because he first withdrew himself."*[19]

Thus, God withdraws his light and in this void, in this liberated space, he creates the cosmos. There is therefore no nothingness, God being everything before creation, but He withdraws in order to "leave space" for creation.

These two examples clearly illustrate that theologians have always been aware of the fragility of common representations of God's attributes and have strived to provide interpretations that satisfy the mind. Their technique, if we dare use that expression, consists of debunking naive representations, which are nevertheless prevalent among believers, in order to replace them with more complex, more scholarly representations that seem to circumvent contradictions by leading the mind into a kind of intellectual cul-de-sac. The image closes the debate.

Thus, the Thomist explanation interpreted by François-Xavier Putallaz and that of tsimtsoum converge in that they consist of beautiful images, but which tell us nothing.

Of course, they do say something, but that something is pure abstraction. We are here in the realm of abstract speculation, taken to its extreme, in which words and especially images are of great importance. The explanation is based on a logic internal to the image, to the astonishment produced by the image. It is beautiful, and its beauty is appealing. It seduces

---

[19] Marc-Alain Ouaknin, *Tsimtsoum, Introduction à la méditation hébraïque* (Tsimtsoum, Introduction to Hebrew Meditation), Albin Michel, 1992, p. 26

because it appeals to concrete notions that we can represent, that is, a mental image. And this representation is understandable, it pleases us, so we adopt it. But in reality, it only translates abstract notions, which offer no representation. Thus, the image remains an image, like a pretty but incomprehensible rebus.

Many contemporary Christian theologians have also addressed the paradox of creation in relation to the question of eternity, such as Canon F. Van Steenberghen, in an article available on the persee.fr website, entitled "*The controversy over the eternity of the world in the 13th century*," in which he attempts to justify the existence of God after reviewing the theories of medieval theologians and various philosophical currents concerning the eternity of the world and, therefore, the problem of creation, that is, ultimately, the existence of God.

He then puts forward three theses:

The first, with an assertion that, in his words, is "*the subject of a truly universal consensus*": "*Something exists eternally.*" The formula can be translated as "*Since something exists today, something has always existed, for it is absurd to imagine that being arose from nothing.*"[20]

The second, which "*seems obvious*" to him:

"*The material world cannot be eternal. Why? Because the material world, by its very nature,*

---

[20] Canon Fernand Van Steenberghen, *La controverse sur l'éternité du monde au XIIIe siècle* (The controversy over the eternity of the world in the 13th century), Bulletins of the Royal Academy of Belgium, Year 1972, 58, p. 282

*involves a series of temporal phenomena. Now, if this material world were eternal, that is, without beginning, the series of temporal phenomena would be infinite, which is a contradiction."[21]*

Hence his third thesis, "*an immediate corollary of the previous one*":

*"The material world depends entirely on an immaterial cause."*

This is a hasty deduction that starts from a priori assumptions without really being able to prove them. For one thing, it would first be necessary to demonstrate the impossibility of a series of phenomena being infinite. It is then deeply abusive to construct such a categorical demonstration without first defining precisely what one is talking about.

The world. But what is the world? Is it our universe and nothing else, or is it what makes the universe exist and what may pre-exist and be its cause, without however being transcendent? Astrophysicists have hypothesized the existence of multiple universes, others have hypothesized multiple dimensions. Whether these hypotheses are unverifiable (will they ever be?), they are no less plausible than the hypothesis of an immaterial origin of the universe. And what do we mean by immaterial? Are elementary particles considered matter or not? And what about energy?

Temporality. What kind of temporality are we talking about? Only universal temporality? Is it unique?

Eternity. A very abstract concept. And if his logic allows him to deduce the impossibility of the eternity of substance, does it allow him to affirm the eternity of the

---

[21] Ibid, p. 283

immaterial?

In order to complete his reasoning, he takes up, or interprets, a "demonstration" by Saint Bonaventure, a 13th-century theologian, which he presents as indisputable proof, by reductio ad absurdum, of the impossibility of the eternity of the world:

*"If the world is eternal in the past, an infinite series of events has followed one another up to the present day. Is each of these events at a finite distance from today? If we agree, we consider by the same token that the most distant event of all is still at a finite distance from today; in which case this event is the first and the evolution of the world began. If, on the contrary, we maintain that one or more events in the past are infinitely distant from today, how can we conceive of the transition from infinitely distant events to those that are not? We are forced to say that infinity − 1 = finitude, or that finitude + 1 = infinity. This is obviously absurd. The hypothesis of the eternity of the world therefore leads to total incoherence: it implies contradiction and must be rejected.*[22]

However, two errors render this reasoning invalid, because in "an infinite series of events" there is no "most distant" event, since by definition the series is infinite. That is the first part of the reasoning. As for the second part of the reasoning, it is not the events that are "infinitely distant from today," but rather the chain of events that is infinite; the events themselves are never "infinitely distant from today." Both parts of the reasoning are therefore invalid and give rise to what is known as a paralogism. As for the equation, the only

---

[22] Ibid, p. 284

valid one would be: *the finite(n)* + *1* = *the finite(n+1)* or *the finite(n)* - *1* = *the finite(n-1)*. It remains to be seen whether Bonaventure's demonstration has been interpreted correctly.

The only acceptable statement is that "*Since something exists today, something has always existed, because it is absurd to imagine that being arose from nothing.*" Any other deduction is a matter of hypothesis.

However, as long as it has not been proven that this immaterial cause (God under the pen of this author) exists, it would be legitimate to think that it arose from nothing and will return to nothing.

On the other hand, the observation that the universe and humanity are evolving towards consciousness and conceptual intelligence, and, more recently, the development of artificial intelligence, would seem to point towards an evolution from the material to the immaterial, rather than the opposite.

Thus, at the beginning and end of this author's thinking, we find the point of view of medieval theologians who, in their search for the first cause, ultimately refer to God as the basis for all their intellectual reasoning. This conclusion is similar to what Immanuel Kant called the ontological proof: the idea of God proves his existence.

Some Christian writers have also ventured into the search for a causal explanation for the existence of God.

# A few Christian "thinkers" to the rescue

Besides theology, there are also many authors classified as philosophers, convinced believers, whether religious or secular, who arrive at the same conclusion, regardless of how they approach the problem of the existence of this entity they call "God." They start from their belief in his existence, which is not a hypothesis, but an intimate certainty, that it is called faith or belief. Then, having reached the end of their reasoning, which is sometimes very logical, honest, and lucid, they make this sudden leap toward a transcendent deity, a leap that could be called a "wave of the metaphysical wand".

This kind of approach, if not to prove the existence of God, then at least to affirm it, whether implicitly or explicitly, is still quite common today.

A particularly elaborate example can be found in Claude Tresmontant's *Comment se pose aujourd'hui le problème de l'existence de Dieu* (*How the Problem of God's Existence Arises Today*, Éditions du Seuil, 1966), who, in some 420 pages, reviews, comments on, and criticizes various philosophical, theological, and scientific conceptions from ancient Greece to contemporary theories in order to rationally show, if not demonstrate, the existence of God. The approach ultimately consists of observing that organic structures range from the simplest to the most complex, culminating in the emergence of language and thought, and considering that rationality cannot be contained in mineral matter before the emergence of organic matter, and that, on the other hand, since science is incapable of explaining the complexity of certain organs, we must therefore conclude that there is an immaterial origin, which is called God.

This closely resembles the primary cause invoked by medieval philosopher-theologians to provide what is known as the cosmological argument.

This approach seems to have enjoyed something of a revival in recent years among advocates of an intelligent design, which is, in fact, nothing other than God. It consists of reviewing scientific discoveries, from the last century to those of recent decades, in order to show that science not only cannot explain everything, but that, on the contrary, if we understand it properly, it provides proof of the existence of God.

Gone are the paradoxes that arise from God's attributes and that gave theologians such a hard time; it is science that is invoked to counter scientific atheism on its own ground by attempting to demonstrate that science confirms the existence of God both through its advances and through the unresolved questions to which it inevitably leads due to the complexity of matter and the cosmos.

Regardless of its attributes and the representations that derive from them, it has been proven that a transcendent intelligence is at the origin of all that exists, and that this is, of course, God. For the rest, divine revelations from religious tradition take over.

Stephen Meyer's book, *The Return of the God Hypothesis*, subtitled *Three Scientific Discoveries That Reveal the Mind Behind the Universe*, is one of the most representative works of this trend.

In this book, he literally overwhelms readers with

relatively modest scientific knowledge with detailed explanations of discoveries and hypotheses dating back to the 19th century in all fields, including biology, paleontology, and quantum cosmology. So much so that the layman that we are would almost be in awe of such knowledge, were it not for the fact that the author's competence in various scientific fields is widely questioned by many American scientists.

If we are unable to understand everything in this display of knowledge, we can at least take away two sentences that betray the author's true approach and his deep motivations:

"*Thus, a theistic God would, if existent, provide a more causally adequate explanation for the origin of life and the universe than any entity affirmed in competing worldviews (such as materialism or pantheism) that deny a transcendent reality and intelligent agent separate from the material universe.*"[23]

« *As I perceived how theism answered many philosophical questions, some of my existential angst abated.*"[24]

This admission of God's usefulness in alleviating his existential anxiety speaks volumes about the underlying reasons for his intellectual journey, which could be described as pseudo-spiritual.

Regarding *the "more causally adequate explanation"* we will give the floor to Antoine Coté of the University

---

[23] Stephen Meyer, *Return of the God Hypothesis: Three Scientific Discoveries That Reveal the Mind Behind the Universe,* chapter 20 *Acts of God or God of the Gaps,* paragraph *Theoretical Justification of Causal Adequacy*

[24] Ibid, chapter 21 *The Big Questions and Why They Matter*, paragraph *A Presupposition That Solves Philosophical Problems*

of Ottawa, who, in an article in the journal Dialogue, Canadian Journal of Philosophy, gives his opinion on Testmontant's approach, and whose remarks are also applicable to Stephen Meyer and all authors with the same approach:

*"Contemporary cosmological evidence derives much of its prestige and appeal from the fact that it explicitly takes into account the 'latest scientific theories.' But this prestige is undeserved, because it is not the philosopher's job to decide on the viability of a scientific hypothesis. There have always been, and probably always will be, theists who ask the science of their time, in a manner of speaking: "Tell me what you cannot explain, and I will prove to you that God exists."* [25]

It is indeed always imprudent to refer to science to justify the existence, or non-existence, of a being such as God, because, on the one hand, research is becoming increasingly specialized, but on the other hand, it is evolving and theories that are valid at one time may be, if not refuted, undergo serious modifications that render the conclusions drawn by various people obsolete.

In this field, some more recent French authors are not lagging behind in reappropriating the ideas of Tresmontant and the American proponents of intelligent design.

---

[25] Antoine Coté, *Claude Tresmontant et la preuve cosmologique* (Claude Tresmontant, and the cosmological argument), Dialogue. 1998;37(2), p. 283

# "God, the Science, the Evidence"

The prize for excellence in this field undoubtedly goes to a recent work, presented as a bestseller, no doubt due to its provocative and commercial title and its popularizing approach. The book is entitled "*Dieu la science les preuves*" (God, the Science, the Evidence), subtitled "*L'aube d'une révolution*" (The Dawn of a Revolution), co-written by Michel-Yves Bolloré and Olivier Bonnassies[26] . A model of its kind.

Their work is divided into several parts. In one of them, they offer interpretations (a pretense of exegesis).

According to their interpretations, the Bible predicted everything, including the birth of the universe and the appearance of human beings on earth. They claim that no other religions have done this, as they merely deify celestial bodies, proving that they are not divinely inspired, unlike the Abrahamic religions. Thus, they interpret the Bible, but are careful not to do the same with the stories of other mythologies, which they take at face value. In their view, only the Bible can be interpreted.

For example, with regard to ancient Egypt, let us quote these authors:

> "*For the Egyptians, the sun god Ra, with the head of a falcon, is the most important of the gods.*

---

[26] It is interesting to note that they are also co-authors of the preface to the French translation of Stephen Meyer's (a well-known neo-creationist) book, *Return of the God Hypothesis* (in French: Le retour de l'hypothèse Dieu*),* cited above, which was included in the collection "Dieu, la science, les preuves" (God, the Science, the Evidence), edited by Jean Staune.

*It is he who brings life to the universe through his light. Born of a primordial ocean (Nun) and the god Ptah, he begets the world and the other gods. He is the object of the most important cults in ancient Egypt, particularly in Heliopolis, the "city of the sun," near the modern city of Cairo."[27]*

For ancient Egypt, the sun was therefore a deity.

Let's try to interpret this: the god Ra, the sun, brings life to the solar system (the universe of earthlings). Born from the primordial universe (Noun) and the Big Bang (the god Ptah), he creates the solar system and other planets.

Another interpretation: the sun is not God himself, but a representation of the god Ra, just as the cross is a representation of Christ (and therefore of God) before which the faithful kneel.

There is a fair amount of information available on the internet that calls into question the credibility of the authors of the book in question, and especially their intellectual honesty when they also claim, among other things, that Judaism is the first monotheistic religion and the first not to have deified the stars and to consider that the personified god was the creator of the universe:

*"For the theologians of Memphis, creation is the work of the god Ptah, who gathered around him the eight primordial gods he had created (thus forming an ennead). Through his word and his heart, he developed the visible and invisible universe. He established living creatures, justice and the arts, the cities and sanctuaries of Egypt,*

[27] Michel-Yves Bolloré, Olivier Bonnassies, *Dieu la science les preuves* (God, the Science, the Evidence), new expanded edition, Pocket, 2024, p. 345

*royalty, Memphis and its temple. Royalty is a reality of the world of gods and the world of men. Thus Ptah is the shaper of living forms, the author of the entire creation brought about by the power of the divine word."[28]*

Without going into detail, there appear to be some contradictions between this text and the statements made by the two authors. The idea of the creation of the universe by a god was already present in Egyptian mythology, which dates back several millennia BC, and also in Zoroastrian mythology. Furthermore, in most theistic religions, there is always a supreme god, ancestor, or prototype of the one god.

It is undeniable that in those times, the mythology of a civilization was largely influenced by that of its neighbors and vice versa. It is doubtful that a mythology developed independently of all those that preceded it.

The authors disparage various mythologies for deifying the stars, but what about Christianity, which sees in the wine of the chalice, presented by the priest, the blood of Christ, and in the hosts the body of Christ, not symbolically, but literally, with some nuances depending on the denomination?

On the other hand, the authors are careful not to mention Zoroaster, the founder of Zoroastrianism, sometimes presented as one of the first monotheistic religions, if not the first.

*"Zoroastrianism, one of the first monotheistic religions, was established by revelation in books*

---

[28] UNESDOC (UNESCO Digital Library), "History of Humanity" (between 3000 and 700 BC), chapter "The Origins: The Gods and the World."

*teaching that God, Ahura Mazda, is the origin of the universe and the creator of order out of nothing, the creator of the worlds. Ahura Mazda is solely responsible for ordering the initial chaos, the creator of heaven and Earth. Every human being is endowed with an eternal soul and free will. After death, souls undergo judgment and go to heaven or purgatory."[29]*

This is confirmed by other sources:

*"The universalist turning point was essentially concentrated in time, around the famous Jasperian "Axial Age" (6th-5th century BC), with the emergence of exclusive monotheism in Israel, science and philosophy in Greece, in India and China, Jainism and Buddhism in India, Confucianism and Taoism in China, bearing in mind that Zoroastrianism preceded it (9th century BC?) and that Christianity and Islam (5th century AD) followed it."[30]*

*"Zoroastrianism, the first religion of eternal salvation*

*While Jaspers placed Zoroaster (Zarathustra) in the 6th century BC, specialists would rather date him to the 9th century, or even earlier."[31]*

On the other hand, the monotheism of Israel was preceded by monolatry, a form of polytheism that recognizes the existence of several gods but worships one in particular, even to the exclusion of the others. :

---

[29] Wikipedia, *Zoroastrianism*

[30] Yves Lambert, *La naissance des religions, de la préhistoire aux religions universalistes* (The Birth of Religions, from Prehistory to Universal Religions), p. 221

[31] Ibid, p. 345

*"Most specialists, archaeologists, historians, and exegetes agree that the religion of ancient Israel was initially a relative monotheism, that is, a monolatry: Israel honors only one God, Yahweh, but other gods exist, and other peoples have several."*[32]

Let us also quote Professor Thomas Römer, Administrator and Professor at the Collège de France[33] :

> *"Monotheism as we understand it, with a single god who was originally the god of Israel, arose late, around the 6th-5th centuries BCE, among the Hebrew people."*[34]

This is undoubtedly why the authors ignore Zoroastrianism/Mazdeism, whose writings may well predate the Bible.

### As for the Bible:

> *"The Bible did not fall from the sky! It was created gradually before taking the form we know today. The stories, laws, prayers, and poems that make it up were written at different times, meditated upon, revised, commented on, and then edited and translated. […] The books of the Old Testament were written in Hebrew between the*

---

[32] Ibid, p. 348

[33] Administrator of the Collège de France and professor of Hebrew Bible at the Faculty of Theology and Religious Studies at the University of Lausanne.

[34] Thomas Römer, *Comment Yahvé, petit dieu tribal, est-il devenu un Dieu universel ?* (How did Yahweh, a minor tribal god, become a universal God?) Art. Le Monde des religions, May 31, 2020

*eighth and first centuries BC. "*[35]

In any case, even if the authors of the Bible or other sacred books had formidable intuitions concerning the birth of the universe, they do not constitute in any way a proof of the existence of any deity.

Regarding another chapter on the apparition of Fatima, the testimony of a crowd witnessing a paranormal phenomenon, or a collective hallucination, is not proof of the existence of a god.

Another section reveals the positions of several scientists, but the personal beliefs of these individuals, however renowned they may be, regarding the possible existence of a supreme being cannot in any way serve as proof of the existence of such a being. The intimate convictions of Albert Einstein bring us nothing, they are of no use to us, as although he was an authority on science, his feelings have no legitimacy with regard to the credibility of a belief.

Another chapter of the book, dealing with the historicity or otherwise of Christ, does not warrant comment. Christ, being a character in a sacred story, is an integral part of belief and cannot, in our view, claim the status of proof.

In the category of evidence, all that remains is possible scientific evidence.

---

[35] The website *"Chrétiens aujourd'hui"* (Christians Today), https://www.chretiensaujourdhui.com/decouvrir-la-bible/origine-bible/dou-vient-la-bible/

If one wants to find a semblance of scientific evidence, it can be found in the first part of their book. The first 200 pages or so can be summarized in a few words: the universe had a beginning and its end is predictable, given that it was born from a state commonly referred to as the Big Bang, meaning that it developed suddenly from a state so small that it is impossible to describe the moment of its appearance and its nature at that moment, and that, ultimately, we do not know what caused it. Because of all this, and in any case... it was created by God... QED...

Theories such as the multiverse (a set of universes) are *ideological* (implied materialistic), God is scientific.

By questioning science, when we arrive at the Big Bang, at the ultimate reduction of the universe, what can we know about what lies beyond? Nothing. What can we deduce from this? Nothing. What do these two authors deduce? God. On what basis? On their faith. On their belief, which is a preconception that guides their entire approach, from beginning to end.

To simplify things, we could say: "There is no solution to understanding the birth of the universe, so God created it!"

The same applies to biology with regard to the transition from inert matter to living matter: we don't have an answer, so it must be God. This is a naive and childish shortcut.

This approach is completely devoid of intellectual integrity: they manipulates scientific data and discoveries to prove their certainty. Not because the data is false, but because it is being appropriated to support conclusions that are no longer scientific.

On the other hand, they do not hesitate to denigrate

all the hypotheses of various astrophysicists (multiple universes, plasma universes, string theory, etc.) on the pretext that they *are "pure speculation by imaginative scientists"[36]*, that they *"have not the slightest scientific confirmation"[37]* and that they *"are not the subject of any scientific consensus... [38]*, when they themselves offer us, by way of hypothesis, if not answer, a preconceived idea that is no longer in the realm of science but of belief, which is, to say the least, pure metaphysical speculation and is not the subject of any scientific consensus, which goes without saying, but also of any philosophical consensus, or even theological consensus, if we are to believe certain contemporary writings by men of the Church, as we shall see in the following pages.

Here we have the exact replicas of the arguments of medieval theologians, which the authors take up and adapt to modern times.

If the world (cosmos/universe) exists, then there must be an absolutely necessary being: cosmological argument.

If the medieval arguments, the ontological argument, the cosmological argument, and the physico-theological argument have not aged one bit, then Emmanuel Kant's refutations are still relevant today:

The ontological argument? It has been formulated in

---

[36] Michel-Yves Bolloré, Olivier Bonnassies, *Dieu la science les preuves* (God, the Science, the Evidence), new expanded edition, Pocket, 2024, p. 116, footnote 96

[37] Ibid.

[38] Ibid.

various ways. The two most famous are those of Saint Anselm of Canterbury (in the 11th century) and René Descartes (in the 17th century).

For Saint Anselm, God is the greatest being that can be conceived, but if He exists only in the human mind, we could conceive of something even greater, therefore God must exist in reality. God, thus defined, must exist.

For Descartes, God is defined as a perfect being, but since it is more perfect to exist than not to exist, therefore God exists.

These two formulations amount to saying that the idea of God implies his existence.

To which Kant replies, not without irony, that a shopkeeper can add zeros to the figures in his account book, but that will not fill his cash register. In other words, the concept of a unicorn does not in any way mean that unicorns exist.

The cosmological argument? Kant explains it to us:

> *"It is formulated as follows: if something exists, then there must also be an absolutely necessary being."*[39]

But, he concludes, since this approach tells us nothing about the attributes of this necessary being, we decide that God is this necessary being. This leads us back to the ontological argument (the idea of God implies its existence). Kant concludes that the cosmological argument is not an argument in itself, since it relies on the ontological argument, which he demonstrates to be absurd.

The physico-theological argument invokes the idea of cause. Since every effect has a cause, there must be a

---

[39] Emmanuel Kant, *Critique de la raison pure* (Critique of Pure Reason), trans. A. Tremesaygues and B. Pacaud, p. 432

first cause, because we cannot go back from cause to cause ad infinitum. This first cause therefore refers to a being that is necessarily the first cause. The physico-theological argument therefore refers to the necessary being of the cosmological argument mentioned above, which Kant showed to refer to the ontological argument, since it designates God as this necessary being.

The physico-theological argument, which is therefore not an argument in itself, refers to the cosmological argument, which in turn refers to the ontological argument. The only possible argument is therefore the ontological argument: we have the idea of God, therefore God exists.

The faith of the vast majority of believers is based on this ontological argument, even if it takes the form of an act of faith: the statement "I believe He exists" can easily be replaced by "I believe in Him, therefore He exists" or "He exists because I believe in Him."

The reasoning of the authors of the book in question is entirely based on this a priori: God exists because they believe in him. Everything else serves only to justify this belief by making science, history, and texts say what they do not say.

Thus, nearly 600 pages are devoted to naively reviving a medieval approach that even clear-minded contemporary theologians abandoned long ago.

Here is another example, among many, that is particularly telling of the biased interpretations, bordering on bad faith, of these two authors regarding a criticism by Celsus of Jewish beliefs:

"*The cosmology of the chosen people was therefore completely iconoclastic* (against the worship of stars such as the moon or the sun [author's note]). *This earned us the scandalized and, in retrospect, delightful comment by Celsus in his True Discourse Against the Christians (circa 178 AD):*

> "As for the Jews, it is first surprising that men who worship the sky and the angels of heaven make no mention of the sun and moon, the fixed and wandering stars, that is, of the most august and powerful things in the sky, as if it were permissible for the whole to be God and for the parts that compose it to have nothing divine. »[40]

First, it should be noted that the text quoted by the authors does not come directly from the "True Discourse Against Christians," since that book has been lost. It is a quotation taken from "Against Celsus" written by Origen in 248. If we accept Origen's quotation of Celsus as authentic, the interpretation given by Michel-Yves Bolloré and Olivier Bonnassies is completely fallacious. These authors seem to be mocking Celsus by interpreting his remark as an affirmation on his part of the divine nature of the sun and the moon, and taking offense at the fact that the Jews do not recognize this. However a more careful reading of this text allows for a completely different interpretation: Celsus does not understand that, since God is the whole according to Jewish belief, Jews deny the divine nature of the stars, even though they are also

---

[40] Michel-Yves Bolloré, Olivier Bonnassies, *Dieu la science les preuves* (God, the Science, the Evidence), new expanded edition, Pocket, 2024, p. 346

part of the whole. In short, if God is the whole, Jews should also consider the stars to be divine since they are part of the whole. This would be perfectly logical on their part from this point of view.

Celsus' criticism is therefore entirely relevant, and he is not expressing his own opinion, but rather what he believes Jews should think, given their belief in an omnipresent and all-encompassing god.

Whether Celsus may have misinterpreted the Bible is another matter entirely.

# Contemporary theology

It is quite surprising to note that contemporary theology is almost diametrically opposed to naive conceptions of creation and the search for proof of God's existence.

Take, for example, Jean-Marie Ploux (priest, theologian, and educator), who, in his book *Dieu n'est pas ce que vous croyez* (God Is Not What *You* Think), chooses to ignore the paradox by shifting the problem of material creation, understood as an act, toward the creation of meaning.

After considering that the question of God is *"Not 'Does God exist?' The answer is undecidable and is a matter of free will. But: what representation, what figure, or what conception of God can inspire this trust, justify risking one's life for it?"*[41]

He then emphasizes that *"We can no longer understand what 'God the creator' means; it is no longer a representation of God that speaks to us."*[42]

But, according to him, this does not mean abandoning the traditional idea of creation. It means that the world has meaning, that God is not the world, it *"reminds us that man is not the owner of planet Earth and that its riches are intended for all"*[43] , that *"creation*

---

[41] Jean-Marie Ploux, *Dieu n'est pas ce que vous croyez (God Is Not What You Think)*, p. 7

[42] Ibid., p. 41

[43] Idib, pp. 42–43

*is an 'act of speech'"*[44] and above all that *"creation is another name for his presence and his committed love so that nothing of each human existence is lost."*[45]

In his conclusion, he offers us, among other things, this admission, which leaves non-believers and no doubt many traditional believers perplexed:

> *"First of all, I'm not sure I believe in God... I love him. I probably love him very badly, but the question of his existence doesn't concern me, or at least not anymore."*[46]

This book, which has the merit of courage and honesty, presents the problem of God and creation in a more appealing light, because it invites us above all to embark on a spiritual journey rather than naively seeking to prove our beliefs scientifically. On the other hand, it reduces this god to a being whose divinity no longer has anything in common with that to which we have been accustomed by monotheistic orthodoxies:

> *"God does not know everything. [...] God does not live in an eternity that would set him apart from time, nor in a 'Heaven' that would make him alien to the world and the earth. If that were the case, we might as well say that he does not exist for us."*[47]

This is a shift from the act of material creation and an all-powerful god to an essentially spiritual god. He

---

[44] Idib, p. 43

[45] Idib, p. 44

[46] Ibid., p. 152

[47] Idib, p. 48

has come down from his paradise to be closer to humanity. Is this really still a god, a personal, immaterial being at the origin of everything, or is it simply a symbol or pretext for spiritual aspiration?

Regarding the attempts to seek proofs, he believes that "*no demonstration of God's existence has ever convinced or converted anyone*"[48] and that "*a god who explains is useless*"[49] .

We must also mention Jacques Arnould, a theologian who, in his book "Dieu n'a pas besoin de preuves" (God does not need proof), strongly condemns this new way of using science to prove God's existence:

"*It is one thing to deny the existence of evolutionary theories and to try by all means to prevent them from being taught in schools and universities: the strategy of the early creationists at least had the merit of not 'touching' science, but rather rejecting it outright and refusing any compromise. On the other hand, to camouflage and disguise biblical texts to make them look like scientific articles, to create evidence designed to make this (pseudo) reality coincide with sacred history, or to hunt down the slightest gap in current knowledge in order to impose a God who can fill it, is to resort to falsification and illusion in an attempt to control one of the most intimate areas of the human person: his faith. I cannot subscribe to such*

---

[48] Idib, p. 30

[49] Idib, p. 35

*maneuvers.*[50]

We would also like to mention the book entitled "*Il n'y a pas de problème de l'existence de Dieu*" (There is *no problem with the existence of God*) by Paule Levert, a 20th-century Christian philosopher who died in 1995, in which we can glean a few quotes and reflections illustrating the views of Christian philosophers of the second half of the 20th century:

> *"The application of the category of causality to God is the greatest source of atheism in the modern world"* (Gabriel Marcel).[51]

Paule Levert adds that this use of causality to prove the existence of God "*betrays the idea of a spiritual God,*" to whom "*it does not provide the intelligibility it seems to promise.*"[52]

She quotes extensively from two philosophers of the 19th and 20th centuries: Jules Lagneau (1851-1894) and Jean Nabert (1881-1960)

Jules Lagneau:

> *"We must convince ourselves that it is not the existence of God that we need to be certain of."*[53]

Paule Levert adds:

---

[50] Jacques Arnould, *Dieu n'a pas besoin de preuves* (God Does Not Need Proof)

[51] Gabriel Marcel, quoted by Paule Levert, in *Il n'y a pas de problème de l'existence de Dieu* (There is no problem with the existence of God), p. 124

[52] Paule Levert, Idib, p. 124

[53] Jule Lagneau, Course on God, p. 249, quoted by Paule Levert, in *Il n'y a pas de problème de l'existence de Dieu* (There is no problem with the existence of God), p. 129

*"Intellectual predicates such as infinity, necessity, and power are clearly foreign to the understanding of the divine; they have nothing divine about them."[54]*

Then, quoting Jean Nabert:

*"The criteria for the divine must essentially seek to dissociate attributes that proceed from a speculative determination of God from those that are discovered through reflection on the assertions of religious consciousness and their implications."[55]*

And Paule Levert concludes:

*"Reflection on the thoughts of Lagneau and Nabert, so foreign to the pretension of posing a speculative problem of the existence of God and resolving it by means of rational proofs, leads to the certainty that this pretension is absurd and vain. At the same time, it completely renews the meaning of God's affirmation in us; it shows that our relationship with God must be incomparably more internal, more intense than it can be through speculation: that it is of a completely different order."[56]*

This is similar to the view of Jean-Marie Ploux and Jacques Arnould, and completely contradicts the approach taken by Michel-Yves Bolloré and Olivier

---

[54] Idib, p. 135

[55] Jean Nabert, *Le désir de Dieu* (The desire for God), Paris, Les Éditions du Cerf, 1996, quoted by Paule Levert Idib, p. 135

[56] Idib, p. 164

Bonnassies in their book. One cannot help but wonder about the motivations of the two engineers, one of whom is a graduate of the prestigious École Polytechnique.

The faith of our two authors has therefore not evolved to the point of falling into the trap of evidence .

This strategy, if it is one, will not fill the churches or bring agnostics or atheists back into the fold. It may reinforce those who believe in God as one believes in reincarnation or astrology. Concerned about the growing disinterest in Christianity among most of their fellow citizens, did they want to work to bring back the undecided or strengthen the faith of believers in search of answers?

It is to be feared that their approach is misguided, if we are to believe Paule Levert:

*"Speculation is incapable of reaching God. He is relative to what we are: to our perceptive activity, to that of our senses and our understanding."*[57]

On the other hand, the authors are careful not to define this God whose existence they loudly proclaim to have proven. Is this higher entity singular or plural? What are its characteristics? How can it be defined?

*"That's not the subject of the book!"* Olivier Bonassier asserts in an interview with TV5MONDE[58] . *"We want to try to seriously answer a single question: not who God is, but whether or not there is a creator god, whether we can pronounce on the matter."*

---

[57] Idib, p. 125

[58] Michel-Yves Bolloré and Olivier Bonnassies: "La preuve que Dieu existe" (The proof that God exists) https://www.youtube.com/watch?v=mDFb57a_S1E

However, on reading the book carefully, it is clearly about the monotheistic god inherited from Judaism, as they insistently point out several times, and the god of the apparition of Fatima. It is therefore the god of Christianity. It is not just anyone or anything. In reality, this god was already there, even before the idea for the book, before its conception, with all his attributes and all his Judeo-Christian representations.

What we can take away from this book is that in order to fully embrace it, there is a prerequisite: you must believe in the monotheistic God and, moreover, have Christian faith. This is why, among non-believers, the argument falls flat. Agnostics, for whom representations of God are still more or less credible, may be prone to some doubts that tickle their conscience, but atheists, true atheists, will see only the ramblings of an almost childish naivety, which will only confirm them in their fundamental disbelief.

These two authors would do well to ponder these two sentences by Gabriel Marcel:

"*The application of the category of causality to God is the greatest source of atheism in the modern world,*" quoted above, or this one: "*That whose existence could be demonstrated would not and could not be God.*"

# Between theism and atheism

There are three main schools of thought that have attempted to position themselves in relation to the concept of deity in order to give a more credible idea of it, or to avoid taking a position.

Let us note, in no particular order, pantheism, deism, and agnosticism as safeguards against atheism, which has always been, and still is today, demonized by all religions and intimidates even non-practitioners who are on the verge of disbelief.

### Pantheism
A kind of atheism that dares not speak its name: God is no longer transcendent, he is immanent. He is no longer a personal being independent of the world. He is the world. The Jewish religious authorities of Amsterdam in the 17th century were well aware of this when they excluded Spinoza from the Jewish community, which amounted to excommunication.

### Deism
A rational affirmation of the existence of a god without being able to determine his attributes exactly. There remains a certain vagueness about the true nature of this deity, whose revelation is rejected, along with all religion. This god becomes a kind of hypothesis emptied of all the attributes of a god worthy of the name. In many ways, deism seems to be a kind of transition from theism to agnosticism.

### Agnosticism (or the trap of agnosticism)

The agnostic does not want to take a stand, remains outside the debate, does not know, does not choose, does not express an opinion, neither affirming nor denying the existence of a god. This attitude exempts him from asking questions.

In reality, isn't the agnostic only agnostic about the religion he has left?

Would they give them more credibility than others? But then they would have to explain themselves, find reasons, and defend them. Ultimately, this would amount to giving them credit.

So when agnostics define themselves as such, which gods do they have in mind? Those of Christianity, Judaism, or Islam, i.e., more generally, those of the Abrahamic Bible[59] ?

What about the deities of polytheistic pantheons: Odin and the countless helpers of Norse mythology; Zeus-Jupiter, Dionysus-Bacchus, or Hades-Pluto of Greco-Roman beliefs; Agni, Vâya, and Sûrya of the Vedic triad or Brahmâ, Vishnu, and Shiva of Hinduism; the gods of ancient Egypt, those of the Mayans, those of Shintoism, and many others, not to mention Ahura Mazdâ of Zoroastrianism?

Are all these deities part of this refusal to question? If not, should we conclude that agnostics have a preference? And according to what criteria? They who

---

[59] And yet, are we not dealing with three very different gods? For some, it is an inclusive god who, out of love for humanity, embraces all humans, whoever they may be, while others make him an exclusive god who chooses his own at the expense of the rest of humanity or who commands and legislates through prohibitions and diktats.

claim to know nothing, to neither affirm nor deny.

If someone can neither affirm nor deny that the absolute exists, or believes that the absolute is inaccessible to the human mind, what absolute are they talking about? What is its definition, what are the limits within which their indecision lies, and beyond which they would classify any deistic or theistic account as fantasy or mythology, i.e., with little or no credibility?

In short, do they have one or more criteria for credibility, and what are they?

Who would dare to adopt an agnostic attitude towards the existence of bigfoots, unicorns, or pink elephants?

No one would dispute that these are pure figments of the imagination.

It will no doubt be objected that we are here comparing two categories of beings that cannot be compared. But that brings us back to the previous question: according to what criteria would one category of beings born of the imagination be more credible than another category also born of the imagination? Would this mean that a transcendent unicorn is more credible than a unicorn of flesh and blood? The latter because its existence must be subject to the test of truth and tangibility, and the former because it cannot be. Would something that cannot be explained or proven therefore be more credible?

It's not that the agnostic doesn't ask the right questions, he doesn't ask any. But in doing so, he still answers it by stating that he cannot answer it, which ultimately implies a question. About what exactly?

In reality, if agnostic refuse to take a stand, it is because he has adopted or retained the representations of monotheism and is often unable to detach himself from them.

# Atheism and what it is not

One of the primary reasons for atheism, aside from a lack of sensitivity to spirituality of a religious nature, is the inability to accept the existence of an immaterial, unique being at the origin of all things, that is, a being that is itself the whole before anything else exists and capable of producing matter through sheer will.

Or to put it another way, the intellect and emotions of atheists are characterized by the absence of mental representations that allow them to conceive of a being as defined by monotheism.

In believers, and we could probably say without much risk of error, in all believers, these mental representations exist a priori. Either they have been present since childhood, in which case they are deeply rooted, or they have found fertile ground in which to germinate, take root, and flourish, leading to conversion.

As for atheists, regardless of the educational context in which they were raised, these representations have not taken root or have been rejected, like grafts that have not been accepted by the body.

For the average atheist, if we can understand them as such, atheism is not a philosophical system, it is not even a system at all. First of all, they are not interested, intellectually or emotionally, in the idea of God, which does not register in their minds. It has no hold over them. It is then that he sometimes attempts, often clumsily, through scholars, to define his atheism through philosophical or scientific considerations in order to turn it into a conviction.. But, a priori, this is neither knowledge, nor belief, nor even conviction, even less a project, but rather an absence of representation concerning an abstract being that he considers to be a figment of the imagination. And finally, because if he goes further and begins to reflect on the attributes given to this supreme being, he finds that, whatever their representations, they are irreconcilable and make its existence inconceivable.

## Are atheists an endangered species?

During the many debates between atheism and theism, there is one argument that is particularly perplexing and often found in the writings of defenders of theism: the assertion that atheism does not really exist, that atheists believe themselves to be atheists, but that they are not really atheists. This is a way of denigrating atheism by denying its legitimacy.

Here are a few examples:
"*Apart from those atheists who deny God because they have a higher idea of him than their contemporaries, there are only practical atheists, whose atheism consists not in denying the truth of God's existence, but in not realizing God in their actions. Practical atheism is moral evil, which does not imply the denial of the absolute value of moral law, but simply rebellion against that law. Apart from this practical atheism, there is no real atheism.*"[60]

---

[60] Jules l'Agneau, *De l'existence de Dieu (On the Existence of God),* (1925), p. 11

*"True atheism would consist in denying, not the existence, but the reality of the absolute. This atheism is impossible; the absolute is always affirmed as the goal toward which nature tends and as the object of intelligence and will."*[61]

We are flirting here with what is called the ontological proof of the existence of God: intelligence at the idea of the absolute, so this absolute is a reality, yet this absolute being God, it is therefore real. However, the absolute is, a priori, a purely abstract idea. If reality there is, it is an abstract reality. Now, theism is above all a fideist adhesion to the reality of an existence, not of an abstraction. True atheism is therefore indeed the negation of the existence of the absolute.

Fernand van Steenberghen, Belgian philosopher and theologian, in an article entitled *The Philosophical Problem of the Existence of God*, available on the Persée website:

*"Firstly, it is possible that there are hardly any atheists in the strict sense of the word, that is, people who are sincerely convinced of the non-existence of God because they have demonstrated to themselves the impossibility of his existence. It is difficult to prove that something does not exist: one can show the inadequacy of this or that proof of God's existence, one can even consider that God's existence is unlikely, given the chaos of all kinds that affects the universe; but to truly eliminate the "God" hypothesis, it would be necessary*

---

[61] Idib, p.14

*to establish that the world of our experience is sufficient in itself and excludes any other explanation, which is certainly very difficult: for either we accept metaphysical knowledge, in which case we are almost inevitably led to affirm God, or we reject metaphysical knowledge, but then we obviously condemn ourselves to an agnostic, purely negative or abstentionist attitude towards anything beyond the world of experience. It is therefore not obvious that there are atheists proper.*[62]

One might think this text was dated if one had not encountered the same kind of argument in much more recent articles.

In response to these assertions, one might say that the problem is poorly posed. The atheist is not concerned with the question of proof. He may, as a mental exercise, examine the arguments of God's existence in order to demonstrate their futility, but he does not have to prove anything. As for the difficulty of proving that something does not exist, one could have challenged the author of this article, if he were still alive, to prove the non-existence of Jupiter, Juno, and Dionysus, or that of Ra, Shiva, Brahma, and Vishnu, or even that of the Shinto gods (what about the Devil, angels, and other jinn?). The atheist is not so as a result of the administration or refutation of any proof; he is, first and foremost, as we will never tire of repeating, by the absence or impossibility of a representation of God and, possibly reinforced by the realization of the

[62] Fernand Van Steenberghen, *Le problème philosophique de l'existence de Dieu* (The Philosophical Problem of the Existence of God), Revue philosophique de Louvain, Troisième série, tome 45, no 5, 1947. p. 7 DOI: https://doi.org/10.3406/phlou.1947.4090

incompatibility of his attributes, which determine a paradoxical, even absurd being, legitimizing a categorical rejection of the monotheistic concept of the divine, and by the conclusion that it can only be a purely imaginary being conceived by the human psyche.

Claude Tresmontant is a model of the genre in his book *Les problèmes de l'athéisme (The Problems of Atheism)*.

Let us cite a few examples:

*"Pure atheism does not exist."*[63]

*"Atheism has absolutely nothing to do with rationalism, and rationalism has nothing to do with atheism."*[64]

*"Atheism is a belief, and modern atheism is essentially fideistic since it refuses to give philosophical reasons for its existence."*[65]

*"Atheism is an irrational belief, and as such it belongs to the realm of psychology."*[66]

*"It appears that atheism has no valid reasons to justify and maintain itself in existence, but it does have excuses."*[67]

*"There is a spiritual hatred of Jewish and Christian monotheism, which is not caused by the corruptions of*

---

[63] Claude Tresmontant, *Les problèmes de l'athéisme* (The Problems of Atheism), p. 438

[64] Idib

[65] Idib

[66] Idib

[67] Idib

*Judaism or Christianity, but by their very essence."*[68]

*"It is quite clear how this doctrine, atheism, could be essentially reactionary, and how it is so at its core and in essence."*[69]

*"It could be argued without unreasonable grounds that the atheistic view of the world will ultimately paralyze the efforts, enthusiasm, and energy of humanity, that atheism will have a deadly effect on human energies. In this sense, it is essentially reactionary."*[70]

One is stunned to read such assertions, which bear a striking resemblance to the rhetorical device known as inversion, which consists of turning criticism back on the person who made it, like a kind of mirror. This is a clumsy technique, to say the least, and it is difficult to see any good faith behind it. Nevertheless, we feel a certain indulgence for this author, who died in 1997 and did not live to witness the contemporary violence caused by conflicts in which religion is far from absent.

Claude Tesmontant, again, in *Comment se pose aujourd'hui le problème de l'existence de Dieu* (1966).

*"Pure atheism is unthinkable, and in fact has never been thought, which is to say thought in the true sense of the word: not merely 'saying' or 'uttering a semblance of speech', but integrating the given, in this case the world. There are pantheistic philosophies in*

---

[68] Idib, p. 439

[69] Idib, p. 440

[70] Idib

*the history of human thought. There is also a non-pantheistic, but theistic, more precisely monotheistic, philosophical current. But to our knowledge, there is not yet a coherent philosophy that has thought about the world from an atheistic perspective.*"[71]

We reiterate here that common atheism[72] is not linked to any particular philosophy and does not constitute a philosophical or even scientific system. However, we question whether there is no scientific thinking or at least scientific hypothesis that has considered the world from a non-theistic perspective. We refer to Stephen Hawking's book, "*The Grand Design*", in which he sets out the most recent scientific theories and hypotheses and concludes that "*It is not necessary to invoke God to light the blue touch paper and set the universe going.*"[73]

Camille Riquier (in an interview for L'Express): "*Atheists sometimes confess that they would like to believe, but cannot, as reflected in Emmanuel Carrère's book* Le Royaume, *in which he recounts his failure to*

---

[71] Claude Tresmontant, *Comment se pose aujourd'hui le problème de l'existence de Dieu (*How the Problem of God's Existence Arises Today), p. 386

[72] What is meant here by common atheism is that of ordinary people, whose knowledge of philosophy and science is relatively limited and who are not the source of their disbelief, which is nevertheless sincere and unwavering.

[73] Stephen Hawking and Leonard Mlodinow, *The Grand Design,* at the end of the last chapter "*The Grand Design*"

*believe. Atheism was very strong in the 20th century. Today, I know few self-proclaimed atheists."*[74]

This generalization based on a specific case is solely the opinion of the author. As for the last observation, it could be said that atheists do not shout it from the rooftops, unlike believers. On the other hand, as Claude Tesmontant points out, ordinary atheism, that is, the atheism of ordinary people who do not adhere to any philosophical system, necessarily remains silent. Many authors who believe, demonstrate it and shout it loud and clear, those who do not believe have nothing to say... a priori, unless the voice of believers becomes a little too loud, the unbelievers must raise their voices... hence the present book.

We must not forget to mention Michel-Yves Bolloré and Olivier Bonnassies, whose assertions and conclusions will always astonish us, sometimes to the point of consternation, coming from two men, one of whom attended one of the most prestigious schools, who stoop to disconcerting childish reasonings. Judge for yourselves from the conclusions of these two authors addressed to those they label with the infamous name of "*materialists*":

*"Logically, a single valid proof is sufficient to validate a thesis. Conversely, to demonstrate that a thesis is false (in this case, the existence of God), it is necessary to prove that all the evidence put forward is false.*

[74] Camille Riquier, interview for L'Express, *Aujourd'hui, je connais peu d'athées autoproclamés* (Today, I know few self-proclaimed atheists), published on January 7, 2024

*Thus, to deny the existence of God, they* (the materialists) *will have no choice but to believe simultaneously that:*

- *There are an almost infinite number of other universes besides ours, because it is today the only possible joker to escape the problem of fine-tuning the universe (they will have to believe this wholeheartedly, even though there is not the slightest clue or proof of this theory);*
- *The first of these almost infinite universes came out of nothing;*
- *The leap from inertia to life is part of the realm of acceptable problems;*
- *Jesus is just an adventurer who failed;*
- *The surprising truths of the Bible are the result of a stroke of luck;*
- *The destiny of the Jewish people is not extraordinary;*
- *The miracle of Fatima is a hoax;*
- *Good and evil do not exist, and therefore everything is permitted.*[75]

Even if materialism is to be equated with atheism, none of these assertions is part of an act of faith that could form the basis of an atheistic doctrine. The first reason is that there is no atheistic doctrine. Secondly, because atheism is not to be found in any scientific theory whatsoever, and because Jesus, the so-called truths of the Bible, the destiny of the Jewish people, or Fatima are not part of an atheist's concerns or musings.

---

[75] Michel-Yves Bolloré, Olivier Bonnassies, *Dieu la science les preuves* (God, the Science, the Evidence), new expanded edition, Pocket, 2024, pp. 557 and 558

An atheist is not concerned with what might possibly exist beyond the universe. Scientists have every right and legitimacy to put forward hypotheses to try to explain the existence of the universe, but this does not concern atheists in any way, nor even believers, who always have the option of shedding light on areas of darkness by using their supreme and transcendent Joker.

So, is modern atheism dead, as Brother Paul Adrien d'Hardemare claims in an interview with Olivier Bonnassies, or did it die a "*beautiful death*", as Philippe Nemo hoped in 2012?[76] However, according to statistics from the Gallup International Association, the number of French people declaring themselves atheists, which in 2012 was up 15% compared to 2007 and represented 29% of those surveyed, rose to 32% in 2022. This seems to illustrate that modern atheism has become a growing societal phenomenon that does not refer to any program, if there ever was one (unless we consider that, having achieved their objectives, these programs have become obsolete).

This rearguard agitation seems rather pathetic, and it is doubtful that it can solve the problems facing modern societies.

The denigration of atheism very often betrays pretentiousness and excessive self-satisfaction on the part of people who are convinced that they have found The Truth, their truth, and who refuse to accept that it can be considered unacceptable, or that one should, at

---

[76] Philippe Nemo, *La belle mort de l'athéisme moderne* (The Beautiful Death of Modern Atheism), Puf, 2012

worst, adopt a purely "*abstentionist*" attitude.

Atheists do not deny that something may exist beyond human experience, but they reject all metaphysical speculation that presupposes the existence of a being, which they consider to be a figment of the imagination, capable of filling all the emptiness of what humans do not understand and do not know, and above all, of projecting onto this imaginary being everything that humanity struggles to express or is incapable of expressing: altruism, benevolence, compassion, tolerance, friendship; in a word, empathy for every other human being, whoever they may be and wherever they may come from.

Faced with this much-feared atheism, could the ultimate argument lie in the assertion that God is the "*fundamental desire*" of humanity?

# God, fundamental desire?

We would not want to end without examining certain assertions that seem to us unfounded or abusive, such as the idea that there is, as Jules Lagneau believes, "*a natural movement that leads men to believe in God*"[77] or that "*humanity as a whole believes in the existence of God*"[78], or, as Paule Levert asserts, that the desire for God is the "*sole, fundamental desire of all consciousness.*"[79]

This type of assertion, which can be found in many writings, presupposes the universality of the idea of God (the capital letter clearly indicates that, in the minds of these authors, it refers to the God of monotheism) not only in geographical space, but also in time and, one might add, uniform in individual consciousness, or to put it another way, expressed uniformly in all individual consciousnesses.

This assertion of the universality of the idea of God raises a number of questions:
-   What about religions whose deities are absent, such as Buddhism, Taoism, and Confucianism?
-   Is the relationship to deities in polytheistic religions similar to the relationship to the one God of monotheistic religions?

---

[77] Jules Lagneau, *De l'existence de Dieu* (On the Existence of God), p. 1

[78] Idib, p. 2

[79] Paule Levert, *Il n'y a pas de problème de l'existence de Dieu* (There is no problem of the existence of God), p. 165

- Based on these first two questions, can we consider that the same conception of belief in God is applicable indiscriminately to all of humanity, on the one hand, and, historically speaking, to all religions since the dawn of humanity, on the other?
- Finally, this also raises the question of the historical spread of faith in the main monotheistic religions, namely Christianity and Islam, but also the place of God in these religions and how to understand the idea of God or, more precisely, the manifestation of faith at the individual level.

The first question that comes to mind concerns the possible comparison between monotheism and polytheism on the one hand, and monotheism and non-theistic religions such as Buddhism, Taoism, and Confucianism, where deities are absent, on the other.

Asia alone is home to more than three billion people, nearly half of humanity, the majority of whom do not practice any monotheistic religion, or even any theistic religion[80].

With regard to polytheism, Hinduism is the majority religion in India, with a population of 1.38 billion. It is a polytheistic religion with countless gods, resembling a mixture of mythology, legends, and beliefs related to animism. In Japan, the two main religions are Buddhism and Shintoism. The latter is similar in many ways to animism rather than true polytheism, through

---

[80] Many Asian countries, including the most populous ones: China (more than 1.4 billion inhabitants), Vietnam, Thailand, Myanmar, Nepal, North Korea, Sri Lanka... to which can be added other countries where a significant part of the population is Buddhist, such as Japan, South Korea, and Malaysia.

its deification of nature and religious practices comparable to the worship of saints in Christianity. It is no coincidence that Shinto places of worship are called shrines and not temples, a term reserved for Buddhism. People visit them on New Year's Day and sometimes for weddings[81] , but Buddhism is the religion of choice for funerals, sometimes regardless of religious practice. Shinto shrines do not have cemeteries (except for a few exceptional individuals such as certain samurai who are revered as gods), which are reserved for Buddhism. Shintoism is not a religion that is practiced at home or individually. Here, religion is a pretext for ceremony; the term "faith" seems inapplicable to the Japanese mentality in general.

In traditional African religions, which are often presented as monotheistic, the concept of a supreme deity has nothing to do with the concept of the personal god of Abrahamic monotheism; it is more akin to a cosmogony. The presence of secondary deities and spirits of all kinds makes them more polytheistic religions or even animistic beliefs.

In the past, religions that did not consider the Abrahamic god to be the only deity were considered pagan, i.e., equivalent to atheisms, as the concepts of god in polytheistic religions and Abrahamic religions were considered fundamentally different. This seems to be confirmed by the choice of etymology for the word

---

[81] Marriages sometimes take place in a Catholic or Protestant church, without any conversion, simply out of a desire for an "exotic" ceremony.

religion: *relegere* (to gather, to collect) or *religare* (to bind, to connect).

While the true etymology is apparently *relegere*, it is quite remarkable that Christianity has always preferred to see it in *religare*, thus emphasizing man's relationship with God:

*"Let us remember, finally, that contrary to what is said and repeated, the primary etymological root of the word religion is not* religare, *to connect, but* relegere, *to execute scrupulously, to gather faithfully. This difference is very significant: while the latter meaning is typical of polytheistic religions, where the most important thing is to do what is right, how it should be done, and when it should be done, the word* religare, *which was put forward by Lactantius (260-325) with the triumph of Christianity, emphasizes the relationship between men and God."*[82]

Monotheistic religions, and Christianity perhaps more than others, place great importance on the relationship between humans and a personal, unique god. Christian prayer does not necessarily involve reciting sacred texts in a group; believers can address God directly in their own words through inner prayer. Polytheism, in general, gives more importance to rituals and chants than to intimate prayer which is the expression of a more spiritual relationship with the deity.

The assertions of Jules Lagneau and Paule Levert also raise the issue of the concept of faith as it is widely used among Christians. Is the relationship to belief common to all religions, especially polytheistic

---

[82] Yves Lambert, *La Naissance des Religions. De la préhistoire aux religions universalistes (*The Birth of Religions: From prehistory to universalist religions*)*, p. 30

religions such as those in India or Japan? Is the question 'do you have faith?' or even 'do you believe in God?' possible when the interlocutor is a follower of a polytheistic religion? Wouldn't the issue rather be to know which god he believes in, and what he represents for him, or even which god has his preference, and what the reasons are, but also to which gods does he address according to circumstances.

Are Japanese people truly aware that they are communicating with a deity when they ring the bell at a Shinto shrine and then clap their hands three times? Or are they simply following a customary practice tinged with animism? Each shrine is dedicated to one or more kami (gods or goddesses of the Shinto pantheon, divine spirits, elements of nature, animals, or even the spirits of deceased people such as ancient samurai heroes who have been deified).

We are therefore entitled to question the supposed universality of the idea of God.

But what about the history of the evolution of religions?

In his book "*La Naissance des Religions. De la préhistoire aux religions universalistes*" (The Birth of Religions. From Prehistory to Universalist Religions*)*, Yves Lambert (sociologist) shows that, in general, there are three phases in the evolution of religions, ranging from primitive beliefs (sometimes considered animistic, totemic, or shamanistic) to polytheistic religions and finally to religions of salvation (Buddhism or karmic religions, monotheistic religions). Belief in a single personal god, as conceived by Abrahamic beliefs, would therefore be something recent in the evolution of humanity[83]. This is yet another argument that seems to contradict the universality of the idea of God as conceived by monotheistic religions.

If we now examine the history of Christianity, we see that it was imposed by the will of the emperors Constantine and Theodosius, and by the destruction of so-called pagan temples or by force of arms, as with the Teutonic Knights who imposed Christianity on Prussia in the 13th century. Islam also spread by the force of the scimitar. Peoples convert willingly, or under duress, to the religions of the victors.

Once a religion has been imposed and established, it is impossible to question it; it becomes the state religion and, even more, the expression of The Truth. Thus, for centuries, the idea of a single god, the origin of everything, became so ingrained in people's minds that the vast majority did not consider questioning this "Truth" in the slightest. This idea is not, and never has been, due to the emergence of individual consciousness; it imposed itself, not to say that it was imposed. Consciousness feeds on what it is allowed to consume.

Let us not forget that certain religions are still state religions in some countries, that belief in a single god remains an obligation in many countries, and that rejection of this belief is still punishable by death. It would not be an exaggeration to say that it is forbidden

---

[83] Let us recall the text already quoted above: "*Monotheism as we understand it, with a single God who was originally the God of Israel, arose late, around the 6th-5th centuries BCE, among the Hebrew people.*" (Thomas Römer, Administrator and Professor at the Collège de France, Chair of « Milieux bibliques » (Biblical Environments)).

not to believe. How, in such conditions, can we talk about consciousness?

So, do the three Abrahamic religions really support Paule Levert's assertion that God is the "*fundamental desire of all consciousness*" or Jules Lagneau's claim that a natural movement "*leads people to believe in God*"?

Religion is above all a cultural phenomenon and therefore essentially social. Before being an expression of individual consciousness, God is first and foremost part of socio-cultural representations. It can be said, without resorting to partisan interpretation, that belief in God has become an expression of individual consciousness, especially among exceptional individuals, such as the saints of Christianity or certain religious figures who have dedicated their lives to spirituality. The faith of the vast majority of people who call themselves believers is often expressed only in communion with other believers, through prayer, song, and religious ceremonies. When believers find themselves alone with their religious practice, it often reflects a fear of the wrath of a severe, punishing, and chastising god, from whom they seek mercy or the fulfillment of their personal and material desires, and with whom they negotiate their entry into the afterlife. Religious practice is often part of a set of obligations which, if not observed, can cause the god's wrath, with negative consequences in the afterlife or social exclusion. These attitudes and practices are the antithesis of authentic spiritual faith and resemble superstition or idolatry in many ways.

Is God really the fundamental desire of all consciousness? The idea of God does not seem innate; rather, it appears to be acquired, conditioned, like one's mother tongue. What is common to all consciousness, if not fundamental, is this triple anguish: ontological[84] , eschatological[85] , and existential[86] , which makes us fear the end of life as the end of the world and, above all, that dull, silent, sometimes unconscious anguish that we can sometimes feel deep within ourselves without understanding its origin and which drives us to seek an impossible antidote.

---

[84] *"No one can escape the anguish of knowing oneself to be mortal and of understanding that everything that makes life worth living - loves, friendships, successes - is subject to degradation and death."* Janine Chanteur, *Écouter l'angoisse* (Listening to Anxiety) (1997), ch. *La dimension ontologique de l'angoisse* (The Ontological Dimension of Anxiety), p. 57

[85] Eschatological anxiety: fear of the end of the world.

[86] Jean Brun (University Professor, Doctor of Letters, Professor of Philosophy at the University of Dijon) speaking about Heidegger: *"It is remarkable,"* he notes, *"that when the anxiety has passed, we readily say: it was nothing at all, because it was precisely this nothingness that caused us anxiety. The anxious being feels that it cannot understand itself from the world and that it remains isolated within itself: we are anxious about our being-in-the-world."* Encyclopædia Universalis, art. *Angoisse existentielle* (Existential anxiety), https://www.universalis.fr/encyclopedie/angoisse-existentielle/

# As an epilogue

The preceding pages do not call for any particular conclusion, as the aim here has not been to demonstrate or, above all, to prove anything, except to show that all belief is a matter of representations that we make our own or, conversely, do not adhere to or are simply absent, and also to note that, if we stick to logic alone, the attributes of God are incompatible with the concept of creation. Theologians have always been aware of this and have sought, throughout history, with varying degrees of success, to produce interpretations acceptable to the understanding and faith of their contemporaries, but they have always, and today more than ever, ventured into abstract concepts and images that are indecipherable to the average person.

For the average believer, on the other hand, this has never seemed to be a problem. In reality, have they ever asked themselves questions? No doubt they don't want to, but above all, they can't.

When the average believer enters a church, mosque, or synagogue, are they really seeking answers to metaphysical or, more precisely, ontological questions? Do they even know the meaning of these two words?

Beliefs are like feelings: they are based on emotions and representations that have been rooted in people's minds for generations. Uncontrollable and resistant to reasoning, they take hold of the mind and embrace as real certain facts whose authenticity may be questioned — if not outright refuted — by simple common sense.

The second reason, which is essentially a consequence of the first, is that for the vast majority of believers, the belief in the existence of a deity is inseparable from mythological and legendary stories, ritual practices, sometimes the identity or spirituality associated with them, and above all the emotional ties that bind the believer to their loved ones, their community, their fellow believers, their land, and their ancestral beliefs. The average believer is generally unable to view their belief from the outside. If they do, it is because they are already outside.

Thus, believers are not obsessed with the existence of their god, or at least they do not make it a priori. They do not start from it, nor do they end up there, because this god is not an entity separate from the totality that constitutes their belief and the representations that underlie it.

The non-believer, or his most categorical representative, the atheist, has generally, in the course of his *disbelief* (if he is not an atheist from birth), carried out a deconstruction, a dissociation of the elements that constituted his primitive belief, to find himself faced with representations that mean nothing to him, or, quite simply, with an absence of representation.

For any atheist, the concept of "god" has no content.

Atheism is not anti-theism, it is a-theism. It is therefore not subject to proof or replacement by another belief, or even justification. It is not a fight or a debate, not even a predicate, it is the simple observation of the invalidity of a concept.

The atheist's representations stop at the spatial and

temporal limits of the universe. As for the answers to his ontological questions (if he has any), he defers to science, sometimes to philosophy, but it is not from them that he draws the reasons for his disbelief. Science is less the direct cause of atheism than of the erosion of representations of God; it explains nothing more than what it has found in the facts that verify or disprove its hypotheses.

As for the initial question about the existence of God, does it still make sense?

Jean-Marie Ploux is right when he writes that the question is not whether God exists, but *"what representation, what figure or what conception of God can command this trust"*[87]. As far as atheists are concerned, they have none.

If God is *"the elusive, the unknowable, the incomprehensible, the unspeakable, the ineffable"*[88] as Jacques Arnould points out, then we cannot name him, give him any definition, or have any representation of him. This is exactly the state of mind of the atheist, and it is not necessarily choosing darkness[89] ... But that is another story.

---

[87] Jean Marie Ploux, *Dieu n'est pas ce que vous croyez (God is not what you think)*, p. 7

[88] Jacques Arnould, *Dieu n'a pas besoin de preuves (God Does Not Need Proof)*, chap. *La foi, entre le Royaume et les ténèbres, Le dos de Dieu (Faith, Between the Kingdom and Darkness, The back of God)*

[89] In reference to the conclusion of *"Chance and Necessity"* by Jacques Monod, quoted by Jacques Arnauld: *"The kingdom above or the darkness below; it is for him to choose."*